BUS EIREANN

A Pictorial History 1987-2006

Ian Molloy, Darren Hall and Jonathan McDonnell

Ian Allan
PUBLISHING

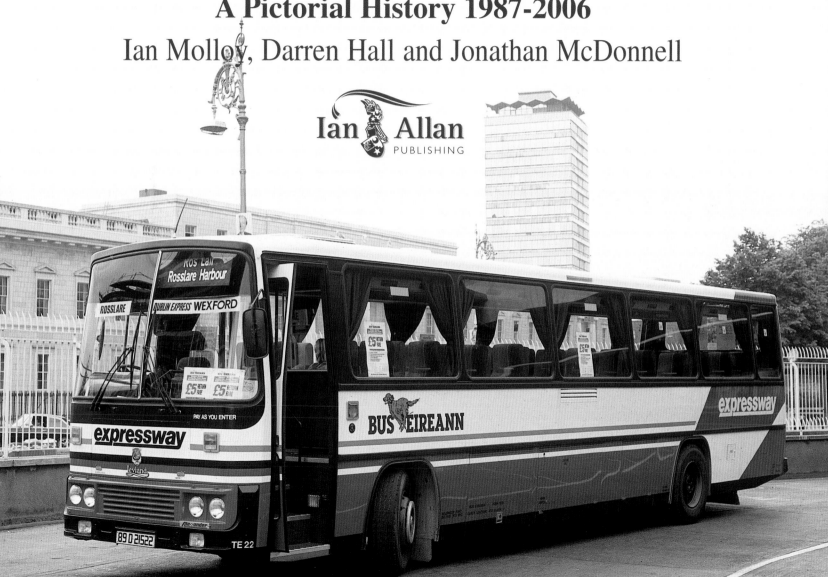

First published 2007

ISBN (10) 0 7110 3230 0
ISBN (13) 978 0 7110 3230 9

Published by Ian Allan Publishing

an imprint of Ian Allan Publishing Ltd, Hersham, Surrey KT12 4RG.
Printed in England by Ian Allan Printing Ltd, Hersham, Surrey KT12 4RG.

Code 0703/B1

Visit the Ian Allan Publishing website at www.ianallanpublishing.com

Introduction

Formally established on 'Vesting day', 2 February 1987 (the date when the 'Provincial' bus services were transferred from CIE — Coras Iompair Éireann), Bus Éireann was given responsibility for all CIE bus and coach operations other than those having both termini within the former Dublin City Services (DCS — 'City') area — these were assigned to Dublin Bus. Iarnrod Éireann similarly took responsibility for the 'Rail' services. These fundamental changes to CIE had been recommended in a report by McKinseys, the eminent management consultants. A notable feature applicable from the very earliest days of the company's existence is that it was allowed to challenge Iarnrod Eireann wherever it suited Bus Éireann. For instance, from the spring of 1988, the former Dublin/Wexford route was extended 9 miles further south so as to serve Rosslare Harbour — previously, the railway had a monopoly of public transport to and from the Harbour. Although 20 years have passed since then, nonetheless many staff within the three companies continue to use the Provincial/City/Rail terms when referring to another company. The common CIE group parentage continues in the background.

As an organisation comprised of six identifiable business segments (Express, Stage Carriage, Schools, Urban, Tours and Eurolines), the reach of Bus Éireann is quite remarkable. With perhaps the solitary exception of north and north-west Donegal, where the Lough Swilly bus company traditionally has had stage carriage and express licence exclusivity (but even here CIE Tours coaches do appear as they visit such landmarks as Bloody Foreland and Errigal), Bus Éireann operations feature in all corners (towns, villages and parishes) of the Republic of Ireland (see the 'Index to Places Served' at the front of the official timetable). This is especially true of the very extensive schools transport activities — there is not a politician outside Dublin city whose constituents are not impacted by Bus Éireann.

To examine Bus Éireann's first 20 years of operation effectively takes one on a quite interesting journey through the recent social and economic history of the Republic of Ireland. During this time, Bus Éireann has evolved continuously both on its own initiative and in direct response to changing customer requirements. This has included such matters as hourly timetable frequency on key inter-city routes commencing with the Dublin/Galway service in the summer of 1998. Substantial sums of money have also been applied towards the refurbishment of bus stations around the country, Parnell Place, Cork, being the most significant single item to date.

Co-author Darren Hall came up with the initial idea for both this and the parallel books about Dublin Bus and Irish Rail. Following publisher endorsement, an intense trawl process got underway. There were problems of abundance in that, when we pooled our three extensive collections of pictures, we had infinitely too many candidate views for inclusion. Given the essential and practical publishing space parameters (85 pages per book and about 100 pictures in total) and also the requirement for geographical and timespan spread, very many otherwise worthy items unfortunately could not make the final cut (perhaps a further book might be feasible sometime in the future?). Also, it was not feasible to include a sample picture of every bus class operated (eg no BA class). We hope nonetheless that in our actual selection we have provided interesting and representative views that capture the essence of Bus Éireann to date.

This book is arranged by reference to the six identifiable business segments as listed above.

Ian Molloy, Darren Hall and
Jonathan McDonnell
December 2006

Below: The summertime lay-off of the school bus fleet in Longford provides the opportunity for this photo. The contrast with the earlier VS class-dominated picture pictured on page 57 illustrates the vast change over the years. Nearest the camera is P12 (ex-Dublin Bus DAF SB220/ Plaxton Verde), then LS119 (ex-G&G Travel Leamington), LS28 (ex-TWM 1181), LS46 (ex-TWM 1125), VC217 (ex-Aircoach Dublin but acquired from dealer stock), LS127 (ex-Maidstone 802), LS35 (ex-TWM 1099), LS18 (ex-Nottingham 742), PL90 (ex-Shearings G821 RNC), P26 (ex-Dublin Bus) and DA5, a former Cork City bus. *Darren Hall*

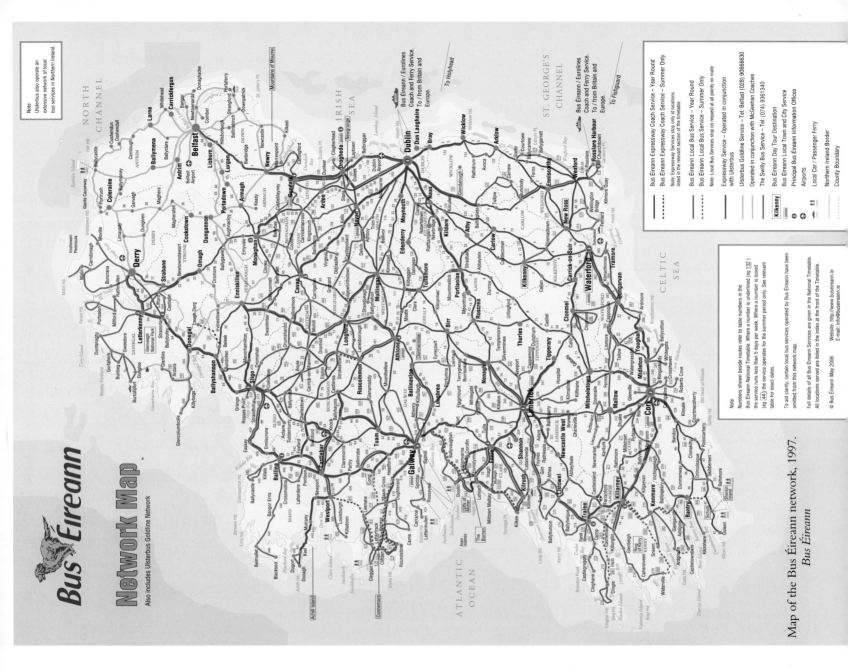

Map of the Bus Éireann network, 1997.
Bus Éireann

Still going strong in October 1987 and looking immaculate is Worldmaster WVH22. The sleek body is mounted on the classic Leyland Leopard chassis. Here the Galway-based vehicle awaits its time in Capwell garage, Cork, before the short journey to the bus station to operate its Express route back to Galway. The photographer wondered how many of the passengers appreciated the finer points of a journey in such a classic machine, a treat indeed! *Jonathan McDonnell*

Approaching the end of its long daily service 64 return trip from Derry to Galway and back, we see 10-year-old CVH12 loading at Ballybofey, County Donegal on 15 June 1996 at about 20.30. The CVH had departed Galway at 16.00 and was scheduled to arrive in Derry at 21.15. This appropriate late-summer evening picture very much captures the twilight stage for front-line express operation by the CVH type — in just a few weeks time, new leased manual gearbox VP class coaches would take over service 64 with VP28 becoming the regular for this specific duty from August 1996. It is noteworthy that both this duty

and one other service 64 overnight within Northern Ireland (at the Ulsterbus/Translink garage in Derry) and have done so throughout the many years of 'The Troubles' and since — remarkably, no vehicle was ever damaged. In addition to being fuelled, washed etc. there, the pay-in of fare revenue is also arranged via Translink.

After replacement by VPs, CVH12 worked express reliefs and also some stage carriage duties out of Stranorlar garage. Later, it transferred to Longford for schools work and was withdrawn in November 2005, being acquired for preservation the following spring. *Ian Molloy*

On 1 September 1995, this then five-year-old Plaxton-bodied DAF loads at Tralee for a service 40 departure to distant Rosslare Harbour in County Wexford. The Cork-based coach retains its original 1990 style destination box and so cannot in fact display '40' but the driver has used his best endeavours (and numerous windscreen stickers!) to clarify where the bus is headed for. PD12 was one of six from the original 1990 batch never to have a modified destination box fitted.
Ian Molloy

Illustrating the hourly inter-city concept first applied to the Dublin to Galway service 20 from summer 1998, we see (appropriately) SI20 heading westwards at Ballinasloe, County Galway on 22 June 2001. This was one of ten coaches (SI11-5 based at Broadstone and SI16-20 at Galway) which operated the route during a three-year lease period from 1998 to 2001. Shortly after this picture was taken, SI20 was returned off-lease and replaced by one of the VC204-9 batch of leased coaches. *Ian Molloy*

Right: This picture shows Tralee's Caetano-bodied Volvo B10M VC28 on layover outside the visitor centre at the famous Cliffs of Moher in County Clare. The VC is working the tourist coastal service 50 from Galway to Killarney (at the same time, Galway's VC5 was headed northwards in the opposite direction). Service 50 is not surprisingly summer-biased with maximum timetabled departures during the June to early-September period although in winter time there is one daily journey confined to the northern (Galway to Cliffs of Moher) portion, departing Galway at 10.30 and leaving the Cliffs at 13.30.

VC28 was on a short working to Killarney only but most journeys serve all listed via points to and from Cork (a timetabled duration of some 8½ hours, involving driver changeovers en route). Limerick is avoided — instead the river Shannon estuary is crossed by open-decked ferry between Killimer, County Clare and Tarbert, County Kerry. Without question, the route passes through some of the most scenic landscapes of the island of Ireland. *Ian Molloy*

Below right: A very busy scene at Galway railway station on 28 July 2003 as this VC loads passengers bound for Clifden and points en route via summer only service 61. Worth noting are the newspaper bundles piled on the dash of the coach — a practice dating back to well before the existence of Bus Éireann, to the days of CIE's provincial services. These bundles will be delivered to small shops in towns and villages en route. Prior to displacement by more recent VC125 dating from 1998, VC50 was allocated to year-round stage carriage service 419 from Clifden to Galway for many years. It was cascaded onto schools duties from September of 2006. *Ian Molloy*

Below: Here we see VC92 at its prime (approximately six months old) on 14 March 1998 outside Macroom depot (see sign on upper right of picture). This Waterford-based coach is working the link from Tralee to Rosslare Harbour (service 40) via Killarney, Cork and Waterford. Driver change would take place at Parnell Place bus station in Cork. With the introduction of an hourly timetable between Waterford and Cork from 2000, service 40 was effectively bisected at Cork from then. In later years, VC92 has replaced KR169 in working Wexford-based local services in the route 3XX series but still covers certain relief Express duties, especially at weekends. *Ian Molloy*

Below: VP35 is pictured here in Letterkenny in County Donegal on 16 May 1998. This is one of the leased batches of coaches that Bus Éireann operated for a period from the mid-1990s until 2006 when the practice was phased out. This coach is operating route 064 from Derry to Galway and is part of a three-day 'link' where the asset is utilised to its maximum. In this picture, it is on its third day of that link. Day 1: Operates service 071 from Cork to Athlone and return, and a late-evening service 051 to Limerick. Day *2:* Operates service 051 from Limerick to Galway and then service 064 from Galway to Derry where it overnights in the Ulsterbus garage. Day 3: operates service 064 from Derry to Galway via Letterkenny and Sligo, and then after arrival in Galway, operates service 051 to Cork via Limerick, and as if that's not enough it then operates a Cork local service to Sreelane at 23.00! *Darren Hall*

Right: On 5 January 2002, veteran Leopard MDS177 awaits departure from Longford alongside then-current service 23 Sligo/Dublin coach VP103. The Leopard had been bought for preservation, having been finally withdrawn from schools service in June 2001, and was destined for storage near Kilkenny city. As M177, the bus also worked the Sligo/Dublin service from new in March 1972. The driver of VP103 (Rory McTighe), seen standing between both buses, is the same age as the M (he was born around the time when the bus was delivered new from Spa Road)! *Ian Molloy*

Below right: Although intended to be confined to schools use only, this coach provided ongoing photographic interest during summer 2006, when it featured prominently on recently-launched service 100X, providing a direct hourly link between Dundalk and Dublin via Drogheda and Dublin Airport. VP104 is pictured exiting Dundalk Garage on Sunday 16 July about to take up a service 100X duty starting from Long Walk bus station. Temporarily assigned for schools float work during the seatbelt-fitting programme, it had been pressed into scheduled use due to severe service vehicle shortages. It was also noted operating service 70 from Dundalk to Athlone.

The coach was the last one of a batch of 12 (VP93-104) which were initially leased from 2000 to 2003 and then re-leased until 2006, at which point they were bought by the Department of Education and Science (DES) for schools duties. From early 2000 to May 2004, it worked service 23 (Sligo to Dublin) alternating every second week with VP103 (see separate picture). It is now assigned to Schools duties near Raphoe, County Donegal. *Ian Molloy*

Left: VG9, a Volvo B12B/Sunsundegui Sideral, is part of a batch of 20 bought in 2004 for Eurolines and internal express work. In this March 2006 view, VG9 is seen here on O'Connell Bridge on service 004 from Waterford to Dublin's Busaras. This Spanish-built example, along with Caetano, Irizar and Hispano Vita bodied vehicles, shows how coaches from the Iberian Peninsula have dominated the Bus Éireann express fleet since VC1-20 arrived in 1994. *Darren Hall*

Below left: SC34, a Scania K94IB/Irizar Intercentury coach. Bus Éireann's policy in recent years has been to buy coaches for tours, keep them for a season and then cascade them to express work, which ensures that the tour fleet is brand new every year. SC34 is seen in May 2006 outside Dublin's Busaras before operating service 007 to Clonmel in County Tipperary via Kilkenny. It is seen in the revised version of the Bus Éireann livery, which it wears well. *Darren Hall*

Right: Dublin Airport provides the setting for this picture, taken on 19 March 2005 shortly after some workings of service 32 (Letterkenny to Dublin) were rerouted so as to directly serve the airport. This reflects both a wish to better serve real and perceived customer needs and also an increasing concern about potential competition. In 2006, some workings of service 30 (Donegal Town to Dublin) and also all journeys of new route 100x (M1 express Dundalk to Dublin) now serve Dublin Airport. *Ian Molloy*

Above: The location is the Diamond, Donegal Town and the time is 08.45 on Friday 30 June 2006. Service 30 to Dublin is about to depart after the intending passengers have been filtered for their travel preferences. Bus Éireann's SP53 will travel a very direct routing to Dublin only stopping at Ballyshannon and Enniskillen and in particular bypassing Cavan. By contrast, McGeehan's 04-D-59533 will travel the 'scenic' version of the route including Pettigo, County Donegal, Swanlinbar and Ballyconnell, County Cavan but will by-pass Ballyshannon. This coach had earlier commenced its journey at 07.30 from Dungloe in west Donegal and travelled via Glenties and Ardara. Another McGeehan coach would have fed in passengers from Glencolumbcille and Killybegs.

This collaborative arrangement has applied since November 2005. Prior to this, the two companies had been direct competitors between south Donegal and Dublin via Cavan. Exactly one month after this picture was taken (ie from 31 July), the McGeehan coach has further extended the 'scenic' version by diverting to serve Dublin Airport. *Ian Molloy*

Right: In 2006 Bus Éireann placed an order for 60 of the SP class, SP31-48 for tours and SP49-90 for express/Eurolines. SP64 is seen here departing Cavan town for Donegal on route 030 when new in July 2006. The service is promoted by sign writing on the windows giving maximum exposure to the six daily services. *Darren Hall*

Callinan Coaches in Galway has being supplying coaches for category 3 work for about six years since a productivity deal with drivers was agreed. Put simply, Category 3 work is hired-in coach and driver with a Bus Éireann ticket machine, Category 2 is hired-in coach with Bus Éireann driver and Category 1 is the normal company coach and driver.

Callinan's coaches are always well turned out and are entirely Volvo, most have BE style LED destinations and they are generally white in colour except for a few in CIE tours livery. Volvo/Jonckheere 03-G-6853 is seen on the Luas line about to pick up passengers on route 33 to Monaghan at Dublin's Busaras on 1 May 2006. *Darren Hall*

STAGE CARRIAGE

Bus Éireann

An overview of Parnell Place bus station in Cork city in October 1987. These were early Bus Éireann days and the multiplicity of liveries is obvious, with 10 buses visible. Pulling away is CIE tours-liveried KE7 bound for Dublin, which is flanked by rural KR133 and Expressway Leopard MG39 loading for Mitchelstown. Also present are two AN68s, one in the former CIE livery and one in the new red and white colours, and bringing some form of uniformity are the three KC class GAC single-deckers. Closer inspection will reveal a classic Worldmaster coach loading for Galway. *Jonathan McDonnell*

Left: A worthwhile effort at heritage conservation saw Bus Éireann acquire former Leyland Leopard/CIE E14 from a private preservationist who had superbly restored it. When the bus was acquired by Bus Éireann it was intended as a heritage piece, but the temptation of running it in service could not be ignored and in the summer of 1991 it was a regular performer on the shorter commuter routes radiating from Dublin. On the evening of 6 September 1991 it was tasked with a service to Navan. It is seen in company with KE26 and TE23 on the forecourt in Busaras. *Jonathan McDonnell*

Above: A wet evening in August 1990 at Busaras in Dublin revealed typical run-of-the-mill Leopard MS158 operating a stage carriage service to Granard in the north midlands. More unusual was the Dublin Bus GAC city bus KC98 operating complete with Dublin Bus driver for sister company Bus Éireann. Operationally the two companies were split but still had the same parent. Bus Éireann regularly strengthened capacity by utilising Dublin Bus vehicles and drivers, but the opposite never occurred. The application of paper stickers indicating the planned journey was widespread practice throughout Bus Éireann operations for many years. *Jonathan McDonnell*

Matching colours in a more-relaxed era. Here Limerick-based Bombardier KD193 in Bus Éireann livery waits its time at Shannon Airport. Also awaiting departure is Air Canada Boeing 747-233 C-FTOD which was flying back to its home base in Toronto. Sadly, such a photo could not be taken so easily today. The terminal has been extended and check-in desks now occupy the same area. Unfortunately for enthusiasts, a small number of so-called 'peace protesters' attacked a US Navy aircraft in Shannon and caused a substantial amount of damage. The resultant increase in security would most probably prohibit such an opportunity today. *Jonathan McDonnell*

Above: A summer 1988 visit to Parcell Place bus station in Cork offered a scene pretty typical of Bus Éireann operations in the city at that time. MG76 and MD117 were both loading ahead of a foray into west Cork, while Bombardier KD182 awaited its turn to travel the short journey to Blarney, a place very well known all over the world.
Jonathan McDonnell

Right: Not far from the southernmost part of Ireland is located a small town called Schull. June 1988 found 17 year old Leopard MG26 about to return to Cork on an express service.
Jonathan McDonnell

Waiting to enter Busaras on 31 March 1994, this 22-year-old had reputedly accumulated over one million miles by the early 1990s, having worked many express routes including the Dublin to Letterkenny service for a significant number of years. Its last few years were put in on service 112 from Granard, County Longford to Dublin. It was among the final group of Broadstone Ms on service work, not cascading to schools until April 1995 and was in the last group withdrawn from schools in June 2001. It has since been acquired for preservation. *Ian Molloy*

On 5 April 1994, Galway's high-windscreen MG210 is about to depart on service 423 to Doolin via Lisdoonvarna. This was one of 20 (M194-213) which were originally finished in 1972 as Tour coaches but were cascaded to express duties in 1974. MG210 had a long and high profile career based at Galway garage.

As with VC50 elsewhere, note the newspaper bundles on the dash and also the TE livery and original style glass-fibre front which it still retains. After withdrawal from schools duties in June 2000, MG210 was acquired for preservation. *Ian Molloy*

This photograph is a classic illustration of the social element of the stage carriage service. The coach is VC139, Limerick-based since new in 1998; it is operating the 'Ballylanders' service on the road to Mitchelstown in north County Cork. The passengers comprise many senior citizens, who in Ireland, enjoy free travel thanks to a decision by the Irish Government in 1967. This view dates from April 2002 and you will also notice bundles of newspapers — late editions of the *Evening Herald*, also daily and local newspapers, using the coach as a means of transport to newsagents along the journey. *Darren Hall*

Plaxton Premier VP92 strays from its usual haunt of the express route to Tralee to operate an evening commuter service from Parnell bus station in Cork on the relatively short journey to Cloyne. Note the conductor! *Jonathan McDonnell*

Above: By October 2000, 10-year-old DAF MB230 PD19 had been downgraded to local and stage carriage work. Here it is digesting a heavy load outside the University College Dublin campus at Belfield, operating service 133 to Wicklow. The service gained a considerable advantage over other traffic by traversing the lengthy Stillorgan Quality Bus Corridor. From joining the QBC at Donnybrook, its journey time would be greatly shortened as it sliced through one of the most heavily trafficked parts of Dublin City. *Jonathan McDonnell*

Right: On a wet 31 May 2000, PL120 (ex-Shearings H916 DRJ) is on stage carriage service to Shannon Airport via the village of Sixmilebridge in County Clare. The first passenger to board the bus is an eager lady in the light blue coat who is about to make a charge for the door! This photo is taken outside the since demolished Spaights shopping centre where a new retail development for Dunnes Stores is now located. *Darren Hall*

About to depart Ballyshannon, County Donegal for Sligo on local service 482, this well-presented Bombardier dating to 1981 was 14 years old when photographed on 8 July 1995. Originally in the *Expressway* livery of orange and red, the bus was now in a version of the standard KR livery. Note the C type destination blind fitted. The main destinations are in Irish — Sligeach means Sligo — with only relatively minor locations such as villages in English, a system introduced in 1966 to coincide with the 50th anniversary of the Irish 1916 Rising. Although initially allocated to the prominent express service linking Letterkenny with Dublin (a significant portion of which traverses Northern Ireland), KE11 was soon rejected by some key drivers on that route and, by special request, Leopard MG176 dating to 1972 was given a minor overhaul at Galway garage and used to displace KE11 to lesser duties. During its relatively brief use on Letterkenny/Dublin, KE11 had a very narrow escape. Throughout the 1981 hunger strikes, property was often targeted for destruction and on one Sunday evening KE11 as the timetabled service car had a trouble-free passage through Northern Ireland but the relief bus following (MG5) was not so fortunate, being seized and set on fire in County Tyrone. It seemed especially ironic that MG5 had worked the service incident-free for ten years from new in 1971 and now, as a relief to the KE, it had been completely destroyed.

KE11 was withdrawn in late 1995 and later sold for scrap to Louth Commercials: its General Motors engine was passed on to a Dublin Bus KD. The 52-strong KE class was unique in that, being so unreliable, none were judged fit for schools use as that would of course entail having them parked away (sometimes up to 50 miles) from base. However from time-to-time some may have slipped unofficially in and out of schools use, usually to cover for unplanned emergencies.
Ian Molloy

Westport railway station is the location for this view taken on 25 June 1996. While on temporary loan from Sligo, the KR has just worked service 441 from Achill Island. This especially heavy-loading route is effectively at least in part the ultimate successor to the former rail system that operated to and from Achill Sound. Reflecting the realities of passenger requirements, the smaller accompanying picture inset shows bicycles being unloaded through the emergency door. It had been necessary to place these within the saloon as the boot space provided on a KR is minimally sized.
Both Ian Molloy

Seen at Newtownforbes, County Longford on 28 August 1999, this ME is working the Saturdays only service 469 from Sligo to Longford. The timetabled journey duration is just short of three hours and most towns and villages of south Leitrim are served en route. Passengers have about three hours shopping time at Longford. Worth noting is the 'Sligo City Service' logo on the offside: prior to the launch of this revamped and expanded network in September of 1999, Sligo had allocated ME204/5/8 and used them as necessary on stage carriage work (sometimes even as express reliefs — see below). The '97-G' Galway registration indicates that ME201-8 were originally planned for use in Galway city but were never in fact so used as necessary union/ management consensus could not be reached with the result that they remained stored for about two years. There was however some intermittent use of ME201/2 on Galway-based Day Tours during that period. Waterford-registered ME209 (similar background circumstances to ME201-8 and registration 97-W-713) soon afterwards became the fourth ME assigned to Sligo city services. In recent years, service 469 has been resourced by 'category 3' hire-ins from a private contractor.

Whilst its passengers were taking the opportunity to shop at Longford, ME208 would have covered the 14.00 service 468 round trip to/from Newtowncashel.

ME205 is seen dressed for express service 064 at Sligo garage on 28 August 1999. *Both Ian Molloy*

1993 saw the arrival of the 20-strong Van Hool DAF MB230 class which were allocated fleet numbers in the DVH class. DVH9 is seen orbiting Busaras, a practice often necessary as the forecourt was always congested. Eventually, after awaiting its allotted time, DVH9 operated a commuter route to Kildare. *Jonathan McDonnell*

What is this 'C' (Cork)-registered bus doing at the Long Walk terminus in Dundalk on 20 March 2004? Replaced at Cork in early 2003 by VWL135-44, Alexander Setanta-bodied DAF SB220s, DA1-10 became available for reallocation. It was decided to cascade these to the Dundalk area as replacements for the remaining PL type on service work (Dundalk was the last region where PLs still worked on service. In the event, just seven DAs were physically migrated towards Dundalk, some via the Athlone hub 'clearing house' system and others via Broadstone. DA4, 9 and 10 remained at Cork where in due course they were converted to single-door layout for schools work. The other seven (DA1-3, 5-8) physically reached Dundalk but there was little enthusiasm to operate them there and so, after some intermittent minor use within 2003-4, they were cascaded to schools work, with only DA1 and 3 remaining in the region. DA2 returned to Cork, DA6 went to Athlone and DA5, 7 and 8 moved to Longford. DA3 (latterly Drogheda-based) was destroyed by fire near Duleek, County Meath in late May 2005 while DA1 continues today as a school bus based at Cavan.

In the event, from September 2004, Dundalk's PLs were in fact replaced by '94-D'-registered Volvo B10Ms VC1-8 11/4-7, 39 of which VC39 was a last-minute substitute for VC12 which could not be made available. With the notable exceptions of VC9 and 10 (allocated to Tralee) and VC12, this then resulted in Dundalk having all the split-windscreen batch VC1-22 dating from 1994/5.

In the picture, which captures the intermittent stage carriage use while at Dundalk, DA1 is about to load up as the 18.10 service 161 journey to Carlingford. The bus retains a full set of Cork city blinds (not of much value here in Dundalk!) and the driver has of necessity had to resort to a paper-type board displaying 'Carlingford'.
Ian Molloy

A very busy scene at Dundalk's Long Walk terminus on 13 August 2005. DPC22 is loading for service 167 to Ardee. Inspector Andy Farrell is about to deputise as driver due to staff shortages — within Bus Éireann, it is often necessary to improvise with either staff or vehicles, sometimes at extremely short notice. This was the sole DPC allocated to Dundalk and it has since been transferred to Broadstone for services such as 104 linking Ashbourne, County Meath with Blanchardstown shopping centre.

At Tralee on 20 July 1996, we see a variation on the low-floor DPC22 above as stepped-entrance small rural bus KR120 attempts to accommodate many intending passengers, at least some of whom are quite tall — but will they all fit? The answer is 'yes', everyone got taken to or towards Dingle. KR120 was one of a few Limerick-based buses which were on loan to Tralee as cover for the very busy summer season. It finished its days as a school bus based in the Waterford area. *Both Ian Molloy*

The DWR class letters stand for DAF Wright Rural, and the class is used on stage carriage services to which the buses are ideally suited, offering passengers the benefits of low floor technology. DWR8 is part of a batch of 20 DAF MB120/Wright Cadets. It is seen here when just a few months old, in May 2001, outside the recently-refurbished bus station in Letterkenny, DWR8-10 are used on local services in this area. *Darren Hall*

It is about 07.20 on Monday 26 June 2006 and VC321 loads in the central square of the south Galway town of Gort. What is remarkable is that all the boarding passengers are Brazilian immigrants who have come to live in the general area of Gort. Most commute daily to jobs in and around Galway city while some travel southwards to work in Ennis and Shannon Airport, County Clare. Others have secured work in the area immediately surrounding Gort. Several Brazilian-themed shops have opened in the town to cater for the rising ex-pat population. The phenomenon has progressed so much that there is now even a local Brazilian hurling team!

Service 434, departing for Galway at 07.45 in its early years from the mid-1990s, was lightly loaded but in recent times has not been able to cope with the numbers of Brazilians wishing to travel so three reliefs now work the road ahead of it, two having come out 'light' from Galway and one in service from Ennis. On the day your photographer called, VC122 was the service car that had spent the night at Gort while both VC321 (pictured) and SP20 had come out from Galway and VP345 had travelled northwards from Ennis. Bus Éireann has responded very quickly and positively to this emerging passenger need/business opportunity. *Ian Molloy*

35

Left: The date is 14 January 2005 and the location is the service 133 terminus just outside the gaol in Wicklow town. What is significant is that the VP327 has completed a timetable link connecting the 07.15 service 23 departure from Sligo (arriving in Dublin at 10.30) with the 11.00 service 133 to Wicklow. In the picture the coach is awaiting scheduled departure time from Wicklow at 13.00. A Broadstone driver has relieved the original Sligo driver for the service 133 section to and from Wicklow. This link lasted for at least a year but has since been discontinued as there is now an extra duty on the Wicklow running boards. During Dublin layover, the early arrival from Sligo (SC56) now covers a service 115 journey round trip (departing Dublin at 11.00) to and from Ballivor, County Meath. *Ian Molloy*

Right: On a very wet Sunday 30 April 2006, SR33 sets down at Limerick station on a service 343 working from Shannon Airport. This is one of nine such commuter coaches (SR29-37) allocated to Limerick since January of 2004 and is unique in that it is stabled at Limerick garage overnight whereas the other eight are all away at various locations throughout County Limerick. Note especially the local registration carried, 04-L-269.

Bus Éireann SCHOOLS

Typical of the very large fleet (SS1-770 built between 1967 and 1973) of these utility type Bedfords once synonymous with CIE's schools operations, SS528 was new in 1970. In this view taken at Ballyshrule, Portumna, County Galway on 27 May 1997, it is nearing the end of its working life — the original glass-fibre front has long since been replaced on overhaul with a rather ugly but functional four-piece metal arrangement. Later class members featured a deeper windscreen. Planned withdrawals began with the availability of the CS type in 1985 and the final three (SS715/47/8) were withdrawn from the Westport area in 2001. At their peak, they seemed to be ubiquitous, popping up almost everywhere in rural Ireland. *Ian Molloy*

The main view was taken at Clonard, County Meath on 23 October 1995. The fallen leaves on the ground confirm the late-Autumn date. This deep windscreen 33-seat bus, part of the penultimate batch produced in 1973, still retains its glass-fibre front. With the exception of two batches (SS1-100 and 701-50) which were short 33-seaters, all other class members were of 45-seat layout. The short SSs were usually assigned to specialist roles, often plying very twisty and narrow side roads where 33 seats would cater adequately for the pupil numbers involved. Significantly, SS1 is preserved at the Transport Museum of Ireland while several more including SS90, 715/36/47/8 have been acquired for private preservation, SS90 being on display at the St Helens Transport Museum in England.

To the left is another view of an SS – this one a 45-seater with deep windscreen and unusual Z registration mark dating to 1971. The location is near the Mitchelstown Caves, on the border of counties Cork and Tipperary and the date is 30 August 1995. The bus was based at Thurles garage. *Both Ian Molloy*

An example from the Van Hool-bodied batch (SS771-800) dating to 1976. Mechanically identical to the last of the earlier 'standards', these had a most distinctive body style and were distributed over the entire geographical system. Lough Swilly even had three, SS777/80/97, on loan from new.

SS782 is pictured at the roadside between Grangemockler, County Kilkenny and Carrick-on-Suir, County Tipperary on 15 April 1998.
Ian Molloy

With patient adherence to directions from helpful staff at Bus Éireann's Ballina garage and after driving some very narrow and twisty roads, this reliable 28-year-old Leopard PSU3/4R was located on Sunday 20 March 1994 on a farm near Claremorris, County Mayo. As with most school buses, the part-time driver was a farmer and CS175 is posed right in the middle of his farmyard with slightly puzzled-looking cattle staring towards the photographer! Note especially the CIE roundel/'broken wheel' on the centre front but on the nearside we have the Bus Éireann logo. CS types based at Ballina retained their former service (red/white) livery with the addition of a broad white band and 'School' figure symbols both front and rear.

CS175 continued in this role for a further two years until the spring of 1996 when it was withdrawn. New to Galway in March 1966, it gave 19 years service there until August 1985 when it was replaced by a KR and transferred to Ballina for schools duties. After withdrawal in 1996, it was sold for scrap to Frank Trainor of Castlewellan, Co Down, NI. *Ian Molloy*

Pictured on 20 February 1993 beside a traditional rural Irish road sign at a town car park in Athenry, County Galway, the driver of PSU3/4R Leopard CS234 has taken special precautions to avoid possible theft of diesel: there is a padlock on the tank mouth and this mouth is lined up with the lamppost — to steal any diesel, the lamppost or the bus would have to be moved! But which of the places displayed on the foreground road sign will CS234 in fact travel towards, Mountbellew, Tuam or Monivea? — the short answer is none, because its planned running board calls for it to journey in the direction of Clarenbridge.

Although as C234, it initially worked out of both Broadstone and Sligo garages (each for approx. one year) in red/white 53-seat bus layout, it spent 27 of its 29 working years allocated to Galway. In the late spring of 1968, C234 was altered to Express cream/brown livery (similar to C253-60 from new in 1966) and had 45 coach seats fitted. It was one of five (C231-5) so treated: C233 and 235 also became assigned to Galway for expanding Express services. Its initial duty was the newly inaugurated Galway/Belfast seasonal service via Roscommon, Longford, Cavan and Armagh. Belfast's Lord Mayor visited Galway to launch the service. In this role, it worked opposite an Ulsterbus *Wolfhound* — overnighting in Belfast on alternate nights. Today, the route continues as Bus Éireann's service 65 and now runs throughout the year on Fridays and Sundays. A variation operates via Athlone rather than Roscommon. Significantly, C234 never reverted to red/white livery: it remained in coach colours throughout its service life and was then painted in yellow/white on cascade to schools. Former tour coach C270 operated similarly in coach colours, but did not alter to yellow/white on transfer to schools work. Advancing deliveries of KRs cascaded C234 to schools duties in 1986 and it was re-liveried to the yellow/white as in this view. During its nine-year schools career, C234 was only assigned to two individual drivers, at Abbeyknockmoy and Athenry, Co. Galway, and the only reason it transferred onto a second driver/running board was because the first driver had died!

Although it received an extensive body overhaul, including a new floor, at Louth Commercials in July 1992, CS234 was quite suddenly withdrawn as a 29-year-old in late January 1995. It is now restored by one of your authors to its former Express coach (cream/brown) livery and seating (see right). It is especially notable as the only C which has reverted to original pointed roof domes. In this case the donor was CS118 withdrawn at Dundalk in 1993. It has revisited Galway many times since its initial restoration was completed in 1997. *Both Ian Molloy*

TEDDY LAVELLE'S

bus
scoile

2 IK

25-year-old Leopard MDS2 is pictured refuelling at Teddy Lavelle's garage on Achill Island, County Mayo. The date is 27 June 1996 and the MDS would just have completed its early morning primary school duties on the island (post-primary schools had already been on holiday since early-June). This 55-seater would most probably have hauled over 80 schoolchildren under the former 3-for-2 loading rule. Note the multi-coloured steering wheel, a feature of several Ballina-based school buses around this time. The bus worked on Achill Island for a substantial number of years and was eventually withdrawn aged 29 in 2000. The driver pictured refuelling it afterwards bought it for preservation — it is understood to remain located on Achill Island. Its earlier express career from 1971 to about 1986 was Galway-based, spending many years with MD3 overnight at Clifden, County Galway.

Originally fitted with a Leyland engine, in the late-1970s a DAF unit was substituted and the bus was re-designated MD. Of the total number of Ms (213), approximately one third each received DAF (MD) or General Motors (MG) engines with the balance retaining their Leyland units. The Leyland 680s removed were then cascaded to 36ft Cs which had been found to be somewhat underpowered with Leyland 600s. *Ian Molloy*

The end of the road. MGS23 is pictured here on 31 October 2001 at its final stage of life before its demise . . . a date with the crusher. M23 was new in May 1971 and operated from Cork, originally as a 48-seat coach. It was re-engined in the late 1970s with a General Motors engine and became MG23. It was then used as an express coach and was cascaded to stage carriage work before becoming a school bus in the late 1990s. This class has become an icon with some surviving 30 years!
Darren Hall

This view at the mid-Cork town of Macroom on 20 July 1996 shows clearly the SS type yellow/white livery uniquely worn by MDS25. No other M featured this and in later years MDS25 was repainted into standard Bus Éireann white/red. Limerick-based P326 was similarly unique in being the only P class Tiger re-painted into yellow/white soon after the first introduction of the Free School Transport scheme in 1967. *Ian Molloy*

Right: By 1991, ongoing shortages of available vehicles continued to be the norm. The 50-strong leased fleet of Van Hool Acrons and Alizees had been joined by the 40 TE class Tigers and the company had begun building up the DAF MB230 fleet that formed the PD class. Even allowing for this and Dublin Bus hire-ins, available capacity did not match demand. Helping to bridge the gap was schools Leopard MS110, operating from Busaras to Kildare on a stage carriage service. MS110 was still taxed as a service bus so it was still able to help out.
Jonathan McDonnell

Below right: Bank Holiday weekends put a tremendous strain on the Bus Éireann network, given its policy of carrying anyone who wishes to travel. The August bank holiday of 1991 was no different and gave rise to an unusual situation. Former RAF Bedford 47AC85, by now part of the Bus Éireann schools fleet, was pressed into service and is seen here operating to Granard, a journey of almost three hours! Procuring the bus was one thing, but finding a driver was another. As the Bedford had a manual gearbox, a correctly licensed driver had to be found. In charge of BM23 on this occasion was a Dublin Bus driver, a 30-year company veteran. The photographer feels the indifferent look on the passengers' faces says it all.

Also hastily grabbed and pressed into service was exhibition bus MDS135, whose markings were obscured by the pedestrian who seemed unaware of the dangers posed by the moving AN68 in the background. PD15 exits Busaras behind BM23 on the long haul to Tralee.
Jonathan McDonnell

Unseasonable snowfall provides the backdrop to this picture, which was taken on 10 April 1998. The location is Carracastle, County Mayo, a village through which the main Dublin/Ballina express service 22 passes. Among the sundry second-hand purchases for Bus Éireann schools use were 105 Marshall of Cambridge-bodied Bedfords which were mechanically quite similar to the SS class. These were classified BM. Virtually all came from the UK MoD via trade dealers, the vast majority being ex-Army but some had originated with either the RAF or Navy. BM34 was previously MoD (RAF)-operated 48AC18, which was acquired by Bus Éireann in April 1989.

In the late-1980s and early-1990s, Bus Éireann also acquired from Ulsterbus and Citybus even smaller batches of second-hand buses for schools use. These became classed as BA (Bedford/Alexander). 1-21, BG (Bristol/Gardner) 1-46 and LA (Leyland/Alexander) 1-38 (BG8 and LA25 are pictured elsewhere). They did not last very long with Bus Éireann mainly, it has been said, due to poor chassis condition arising from use of salt for road gritting in Northern Ireland. Space limitations have prevented including a BA-type picture but these were externally very similar to the LAs. *Ian Molloy*

Seen near Oran in central County Roscommon, LA25 was one of 38 similar used buses that were acquired from Ulsterbus in the early 1990s, this one arriving in March 1991. Formerly numbered 1966 in the Ulsterbus fleet, its original registration was NOI 1966. The LAs did not have a very long career with Bus Éireann, mainly due to significant chassis corrosion caused by the manner in which roads are gritted within Northern Ireland. Longford-based LA25 was in fact one of the last operating in service. Although not readily apparent from the picture, coach seats are fitted – these had come from Bombardier KE52 which had been withdrawn in 1996. *Ian Molloy*

Above: Fresh from their long voyage from Singapore, several VS class buses await their new life on the quayside in Dublin Port, having been driven off the *Nosac Explorer*. Jonathan McDonnell

Right: Seen near Lough Arrow, Boyle, County Roscommon, on 12 October 1997, this view shows the former Singapore Bus Service (SBS) vehicle in a very typical rural Irish location with a backdrop of a narrow country lane in the west of Ireland and the farmer-bus driver's house/farmyard in background of green hilly landscape. Very, very different to landscape and climate of Singapore! In a quite unusual transaction, approximately 335 New Zealand Motor Works-bodied Volvo B57s migrated to Ireland, 331 of these were duly modified to local requirements and assigned almost throughout Ireland (County Donegal was an exception although VS128-30 were on paper briefly allocated there but never in fact there physically) to replace the final 330 or so SS-type Bedfords. These Volvo buses had become surplus within SBS because of a local regulation stipulating a 12-year maximum age for PSVs. So the initial 135 VSs dating from 1981 reached Dublin in late 1993 with newer batches following until the 1984 batch which arrived in Ireland during 1996.

VS250 was formerly SBS 4874 and was registered SBS 4874U, new in August 1983. The bus was assigned to this driver and duty serving schools at Boyle for many years, until it was withdrawn in spring 2004. It was later sold as scrap to Erin Recycling, Kinlough, County Leitrim. *Ian Molloy*

Left and below left: Seen at Summerhill, County Meath, on 6 December 2003, this wintertime view clearly shows the rebuilt nearside bodywork (no centre doors and one door removed at front entrance). The lower view shows the nearside rear.

In contrast to KCS202 which migrated from Donnybrook to Tralee, KCS144 relocated from Capwell garage, Cork to the east coast Broadstone schools area. It was one of the substantial UZG-registered batch (KC124-36/40-55/7-72) which dominated Cork city and commuter services from the mid-1980s through to 2000 (see also elsewhere the picture of KC128 taken near Parnell Place bus station, Cork). *Both Ian Molloy*

Above right: During spring 2001, in the context of confirmed UK outbreaks at that time, of necessity Ireland was taking precautions against a potential foot and mouth disease outbreak, so school buses parked within farmyards were therefore totally out of bounds. That just left those at roadsides available to photograph, one of which was located in a remarkably remote spot on the Dingle peninsula in County Kerry. The winding mountain road leading to the parking spot was so narrow that the bus had to drag along encroaching bushes and briars from both sides — in fact just before coming on the bus, one of your authors was beginning to conclude that in fact no bus could possibly negotiate the road and then suddenly it presented itself tucked into the wilderness!

The date is 18 March 2001 and the bus is KCS202 — the last numerically of that class, though KC173 was in fact the last ever produced. This former Dublin Bus single-decker had been withdrawn from Donnybrook Garage in November 2000, following indirect replacement by an AV class Volvo B7TL. After schools conversion (removal of centre doors and application of Bus Éireann white/red livery etc.) at Louth Commercials, it was despatched far away from Donnybrook and put in a subsequent schools career in County Kerry lasting about four years in total.

After final withdrawal in 2005, KCS202 was acquired for preservation and is now once again located in the vicinity of Dublin. *Ian Molloy*

Right: Taken at Roscrea, County Tipperary, on 16 March 2000, 14-year-old CVS9 is acting as auxiliary to Stranorlar's VP55 which is working service 71 to the 'Interlink Ireland' hub in Athlone. The use of a Donegal-based coach such as VP55 was as part of a 'three-day link': on day 1, VP55 traversed the entire length of Ireland from Derry to Cork, a back-to-back arrangement of services 64 and 51, then on day 2 it would cover a round trip on service 71 (Cork to Athlone) followed by a service 51 (Cork to Limerick portion only) and then day 3 would see it return to Derry from Limerick on combined services 51 and 64. With the staff productivity deal of 2000, this link ceased and Derry-based Donegal coaches are no longer seen in Cork.

Because of the imminent St Patrick's Day school holiday arrangements, the CVS would not be required for schools duties that afternoon/evening. The practice of using school buses and their drivers as weekend Express auxiliaries continues to be quite widespread within Bus Éireann and makes much sense in terms of organisational resource allocation. At certain times, especially bank holidays, exceptional demands are placed on available resources, given the company policy of catering for all those who wish to travel. Later on that day, one of your authors witnessed at Limerick a total of eight coaches, one timetabled service car and no fewer than seven auxiliaries or 'reliefs', at least some of which were 'borrowed' school buses, arriving at Limerick from Galway on service 51!

Previously classified CVH9, it was initially based at Limerick for CIE Tours and afterwards Express usage. The bus was withdrawn in November 2005. *Ian Molloy*

Left: A bleak winter view taken on 8 December 2003 near Beltra, County Sligo. This is a typical school bus roadside scene: unwashed for very many weeks and looking generally abandoned. CVS29 spent its entire schools career (from September 1999 through to November 2005) based at this location. When new, it was allocated to Waterford and worked the Dungarvan/Dublin express service for which it carried prominent side branding 'Daily Coach Service etc'. Since withdrawal, it has been acquired for preservation. *Ian Molloy*

Right: EVS10, a 1986 Van Hool Alizee T815 school bus, is pictured here in Innishannon, County Cork, in April 2004. CIE leased 15 of this class from 1986 on and Bus Éireann purchased them from their lessors some years later. This class operated the cross channel Supabus service now known as Eurolines. Cork painted this and other members of its school fleet in this simplified red and white livery, which suits them quite well. EVS10 was withdrawn in 2005 based on age and it was acquired for preservation in the same year. *Darren Hall*

Left: PDS3 is seen near Tarmonbarry, County Roscommon in the north Irish midlands. It is parked outside its driver's house on the roadside of the main Dublin-Castlebar road. The PD class, DAF MB220/Plaxton Paramount 3500 Mk IIIs, were among the first coaches to carry this striking livery introduced in 1989. This view is typical, taken in February 2006 complete with road spray! These coaches were among the hardest working in the earlier years of Bus Éireann and the remaining 57 out of 60 are all on school bus duties, allocated to every garage except Tralee and Stranorlar. *Darren Hall*

Above: Former Dublin Bus DAF SB220/Plaxton Verde P33 (93-D-3033) is seen at a disused school in Carbally near Ahascragh, Ballinasloe in east County Galway in April 2006. This school, built in 1881, is now a community centre and the bus is parked here for its safe location. The entire batch of the P class (P1-40) was sold to Bus Éireann in 2003, having spent 10 years in service with Dublin Bus at Phibsboro, launching the City Swift concept in 1993. Galway area has nine, P30-38, which can be found in normal revenue earning service for the Galway race week in July. These buses are outbased from Waterford, Cavan, Longford, Athlone, Thurles, Galway and Limerick garages. *Darren Hall*

Taken at Knock Airport, County Mayo on 24 April 2004, this is significant as being the only LS class Lynx to work stage carriage (other than occasional unplanned emergency use). Service 449 provides a link between Knock Airport and Charlestown, County Mayo, where passengers can connect with express services 22, 64 and 66. In early 2006, Optare Excel OP4 replaced LS145 on this duty and the latter is now assigned to conventional schools duties within Mayo. LS145 was formerly 1248 in the Travel West Midlands (TWM) fleet. *Ian Molloy*

Above: This mid-summer view taken at Longford garage on 10 August 2002 conveys the annual holiday 'fish-bone' layout used while much of the schools fleet is taken in to garages for both maintenance and also security reasons in cases where buses are literally parked along roadsides or in town/village car parks rather than in private farmyards.

Of the eight buses included, seven are VS type (amply showing how standard the VS had become) and one of these is of the earlier square domed variety (VS2-175) which, by 2002, were in course of being phased out quite quickly. The final bus shown is a KS. See elsewhere a contrasting but similar summer 2006 view. *Ian Molloy*

Right: OP12, an Optare Excel 11.5m low-floor single-deck, the first of its kind for schools. It is part of a batch which came from the Go Ahead Group in north east England. This bus is the former 8136 (R836 NRG), displaced there by new Volvos and Scanias. It is seen here in June 2005 in the Fatima housing estate in Dundalk on a local town service. Bus Éireann also operates these in Drogheda, Sligo, Navan, Athlone and Balbriggan. Although a school bus, the summer lay-off provides the opportunity to utilise this bus for service due to vehicle shortages. *Darren Hall*

As with VC220, this coach was acquired for schools fleet upgrade purposes following the Navan crash. It had previously operated on a three-year lease to Bus Éireann from 2000 to 2003 and in 2006 was acquired for a second time and re-united with its former registration and fleet number. Previously Cork-based, it worked service 8 to Dublin daily, almost always the 10.00 departure ex-Cork and the matching 16.00 return from Dublin. It is pictured on a farm at Calry, County Sligo, on Wednesday 28 June 2006. Note especially the pile of wool nearby — the farmer driver had been busily shearing sheep when the photographer called!

Between 2003 and 2006, SI59 worked for National Express, Heathrow and was registered W895 UVV. *Ian Molloy*

Above: Taken at Ballitore (near Athy), County Kildare on 10 June 2006, this Caetano Enigma-bodied manual gearbox Volvo B10M was formerly Aircoach C13. It is one of a batch of five similar coaches (VC216-20) acquired to upgrade the schools fleet following the May 2005 Navan crash. These fleet upgrade coaches have been directly funded by the Department of Education and Science rather than by Bus Éireann and so wear a distinguishing plain white livery with 'bus scoile' logos. As Aircoach C13, this vehicle operated on lease in Dublin from 2000 until 2004 after which it returned off-lease to the UK where it was registered X393 RBD. It was once again available for acquisition in April 2006. *Ian Molloy*

Above: Following on from the Navan tragedy (on 23 May 2005, five schoolgirls were killed in a crash near Navan, County Meath, which shocked the nation) the decision was made at Government level to phase out the 3-for-2 seating rule and to install seat belts on school buses. Arising from this Bus Éireann bought some used coaches from dealers in Britain. VP406, previously owned by Bebb Travel of Llantwit Fadre where it was registered CN51 XNU, is one of a batch of six acquired for schools, all fitted with seat belts. It is pictured in the village of Jamestown, County Leitrim, a county in the west of Ireland with the lowest population (28,837 at the 2006 census), on 16 May 2006. This coach is allocated to Longford garage for maintenance but spends term time out based here. *Darren Hall*

Bus Éireann placed orders for four small batches of school buses (each batch comprised five vehicles) which would be compared for suitability and overall performance in regional centres throughout the network. Eurocoach-bodied Mercedes, BMC, Irisbus and Alexander Dennis Enviro 300 were chosen and, based on the success of the best type, an order would be placed. Enviro AS3 is seen here on 16 August 2006 after delivery, devoid of number plates. This is the first time since the late 1970s that brand new purpose-built school buses have been bought – the policy until recently was to use cascaded service buses and coaches and to buy secondhand. A further 30 new school buses from the same four sources were due to enter service in early 2007. *Darren Hall*

Bus Éireann URBAN

Right: Wearing the old CIE livery, Van Hool McArdle-bodied AN68 D649 traverses Patrick Street in Cork. The hastily-applied Bus Éireann stickers confirm the change of ownership. The relocated antenna, very much a feature of Cork double-deckers, is evident in this late-1987 photograph. This feature was to facilitate access to the service shed in Capwell depot, which has a low roof. The career of D649 in Cork was drawing to a close as shortly afterwards, it was transferred to Dublin for further service, being displaced from Cork by a KC class vehicle. *Jonathan McDonnell*

Below right: Bus Éireann, like Dublin Bus, lost no time in extending its new corporate livery. D702, a Van Hool McArdle-bodied AN68 dating from 1975, looks smart after repainting in to the new livery, complete with the then-new red setter corporate logo. It is seen on Patrick Street in Cork city centre on route 8 towards Lotabeg.
Jonathan McDonnell

Left: A typical view of a Cork 'standard' on 8 March 1997, when KC128 worked route 2 towards the suburb of Blackrock on Cork's southside. Notice especially the alcopop advert on one of the background noticeboards. These drinks were a highly publicised phenomenon in Ireland about 10 years ago. Passengers are loading at a stop just beside the rear of Parnell Place bus station. By 2005, this had been re-developed such that the rear area had been transformed into the main arrivals and departures point and all the bus station had been completely modernised.

There is also a picture of KCS144 at Summerhill, County Meath while working as a school bus. Unlike many other former Cork city KCs, such as 144, on withdrawal KC128 did not receive a further lease of life as a school bus. Due to physical condition, it was instead withdrawn and sold for scrap. *Ian Molloy*

Left: KD49 looks smart in its freshly applied Bus Éireann livery. This 1987 view shows the bus operating Cork city route 8 to Lotabeg, turning into Patrick Street from Grand Parade. *Jonathan McDonnell*

Right: Bombardier double-deck KD176 is still in CIE green livery with Bus Éireann stickers applied to signal the change of owner in 1987 whilst working on Cork's route 2, still with a conductor. *Jonathan McDonnell*

Below right: In October that year, the bus is shown at the workshops of Bus Éireann's Capwell garage in the process of receiving the new corporate red and white livery. *Jonathan McDonnell*

Just departing Waterford's new bus station destined for the Ardkeen village area, situated adjacent to Waterford's Ardkeen hospital, we see KR168 on 27 May 2000 fully 'wrapped' for 7UP beverages. At busy times, it has often been necessary to use KRs on Waterford City Services. A few years earlier, in the mid-nineties, both this and similar KR109 received a livery equivalent to that on Cork's DAs — they also had seating fitted which closely resembled those of the DA. Both KRs were afterwards used on schools duties, KS109 at Thurles and KS168 Waterford-based, but are now withdrawn from service. *Ian Molloy*

DD27, a Drogheda-based East Lancs Vyking-bodied Volvo B7TL, is heading in-bound on Dublin's Abbey Street, outside the Irish Life Assurance complex on route 101. Bus Éireann now has 23 double-decks after buying 6 in 2001 for commuter services based at Broadstone such as to Ashbourne and Kildare. Following on from the initial success, they bought 14 in 2004 (DD17-30) and three more (DD31-33) in a special green livery for a dedicated park and ride service in Cork run on behalf of the City Council from Lapps Quay to a modern purpose-built car park in Black Ash on the outskirts of the city, as illustrated by the lower picture of DD31 negotiating Clontarf bridge en route to Black Ash. *Both Darren Hall*

Left: DPC24, a Dennis Dart/Plaxton Pointer, makes its way along Merchants Quay in Cork City during 2004. Bus Éireann has 32 of the DPC class, DPC1-21 bought in 2000 and DPC22-32 in 2002; they are allocated to Galway (16), Waterford (2), Athlone (2), Cork (11), and Broadstone has DPC22 for local routes serving such places as Ashbourne and Balbriggen. You will notice on the cove panels that Bus Éireann is promoting its e-mail address and website for general information and to buy tickets on line, a feature of the 21st century information super highway to which every company worth its salt subscribes. This bus was destroyed during 2006. *Darren Hall*

Below left: Leased Dennis Dart/East Lancs DPL6 was allocated to Galway as cover pending delivery of Mercedes Citaro MC class. These buses were leased only for a short period. *Jonathan McDonnell*

Right: This 1 November 2000 view, with Christmas street decorations, shows the then near-new DWM011 in Limerick's O'Connell Street. Note that the bus is in fact TPO, or crew-operated: the conductor is standing near the entrance door organising his ticket machine. DWM001-15 are Wright Cadet-bodied DAF SB120s and all were new to Limerick but three, DWM013-5, were loaned to Galway in 2004/5. Two of these have since returned to Limerick but DWM015 remains in use at Galway. Limerick city routes are numbered within a 3XX range — here the bus is on route 308 destined for the Raheen suburb. *Ian Molloy*

To cater for booming expansion nationwide as the country was experiencing a high rate of economic growth in the late 1990s and early 2000s, the transport infrastructure had to expand correspondingly. Both Bus Éireann and Dublin Bus considerably enlarged and modernised their fleets during that period. 2000 was a year of tremendous expansion with many new buses, and indeed classes, appearing on the streets. Typical of that period is new Mercedes Citaro MC6 seen in Limerick when only a few weeks old. *Jonathan McDonnell*

Below: This unusual picture, taken at Galway bus station in January 2000, shows VWL5, one of four initially allocated to Galway and about to transfer permanently to Cork, with the transfer effected by having the VWL work a relief on express service 51 via Limerick. The rear saloon area was used to pile suitcases and other necessary luggage arising. This was a very sensible and cost effective way to manage the transfer – most probably a Limerick or Cork driver would have taken over the bus at Limerick station.

As a footnote, in attempting to deliver two of these buses new from Wrights, Ballymena, to Galway garage, contracted drivers misread their maps and available road signs, travelled through Sligo and ended up at Ballina garage, County Mayo instead of Galway! *Ian Molloy*

Below right: This rear view taken on 29 April 2006 conveys something of the distinctly Cork character that is especially noticeable to outsiders when visiting Cork. Local people regard (indeed many firmly believe) that Cork is 'the Real Capital'! Corkonians usually finish sentences with either the word 'boy' or 'girl', which act as a sort of confirmation to whatever has preceded. Despite the very local appeal of the 'mega-rear', it is interesting to note that radio station Red FM is in fact owned by UTV, the Belfast-based TV and radio operator.

The VWL is typical of the very large batch of Wright-bodied Volvos that have dominated Cork city services in recent years. Apart from B10Bs VW1-9, new in 1997, all these are low-floor. With the notable exception of VWL2-5 (see separate photo), all recent deliveries for Cork city have been registered locally such as 00-C-28215 on VWL105.

On the right-hand side background, we can catch a glimpse of the Father Matthew statue, a landmark in Cork's Patrick's Street. For many years, the Irish version of this, Dealbh, was displayed prominently on many Cork buses — it denoted a short working, to city centre only, for a bus. Most Cork routes are cross-city. *Ian Molloy*

VWL126 is seen crossing the Brian Boru bridge over the river Lee in Cork city operating the busy route 8 (Lotabeg to Bishopstown) on 18 October 2002. The majority of the Cork city fleet is of Volvo/Wright combination, this particular type (VWL120-144) having Volvo B7BLE chassis and Wright Solar body being introduced between 2001 and 2004. *Darren Hall*

Bus Eireann TOURS

Taken near Moll's Gap, a very well known staging point on the 'Ring of Kerry' tourist trail, on 20 September 1998, this view is representative of the period 1997 to 1999 when VC58-78, 80, (joined from 1998 by VC144-7) were active on CIE Tours assignments. VC58, 63-71, 146/7 were Broadstone-based while the others (VC59-62, 72-8, 80, 144/5) worked out of Limerick. The main batch comprising VC58-77 had an additional centre nearside doorwell (similar to those on DVH1-20 earlier). From mid-summer 1999, the MH class displaced these VCs on to Express and Stage Carriage duties. The MHs were in turn displaced by Scanias SC1-18 in 2001. *Ian Molloy*

Left: VP337 is seen in Galway city centre after returning from a day tour of Connemara, a scenic area in the west of the county. This coach is wearing the latest version of the express livery, which is applied to a minority of the class.

In 2000, Bus Éireann bought 46 Plaxton Excalibur-bodied Volvo B10Ms (VP301-39/41-7) which enhanced services and improved passenger comfort. Today they are largely on stage carriage work although they can still appear on express work as needs dictate. *Darren Hall*

Right: With helpful driver/guide Peter Kennedy standing at the entrance door, Galway's 57-seat VR52 is pictured in July 2004 near Maam Cross, County Galway just after a passenger photography break while working the Connemara Day Tour.

This westbound tour, along with the equivalent to the Burren area south of Galway, has always been popular with visitors (there were almost 40 passengers on board VR52 when photographed). This was one of three VRs allocated to Galway from new in 2000: in late summer 2005, all three were exchanged with Broadstone's 53-seat VC141/6/7. The 57-seat VRs now work commuter services radiating to and from Dublin. After transferring to Galway, VC146 was completely destroyed in a late-2005 fire near Kinvara, County Galway. *Ian Molloy*

While most CIE Tours activity is centred around March to October, there are some round-Ireland tours scheduled during the winter months. Limerick's SP8 was working such a tour when photographed at Glendalough, County Wicklow on 13 November 2005. Starting with the batch VC301-18 dating from 2003, a policy of cascading tour coaches to Express after just one season's high-profile work has been applied. In 2004, SC28-45 were delivered, replacing the VCs, and these were in turn displaced by SP1-18 in 2005. 2006 saw SP31-48 displacing the earlier SPs.

SP8 now works front-line Express, either service 12 Limerick to Dublin or service 51 Cork to Galway. *Ian Molloy*

OT1, former UK registration number S850 DGX, is an East Lancs-bodied Volvo Olympian, the only one in the fleet. It operates in Cork on a city tour and also to the world famous Blarney stone. This bus is also available for parading victorious sporting teams in the Munster region, such as the Heineken Cup winning rugby team in 2006 and is seen in August that year. It replaced Van Hool McArdle bodied Leyland Atlantean AN68/1R DF795. *Darren Hall*

Bus Éireann EUROLINES

A 1992 view of Victoria Coach Station in London shows Broadstone-based DAF MB230 PD60 loading for Ballina in the west of Ireland. A contracted KMP Llanberis driver will take the coach northwards over the 285 miles to Holyhead docks in North Wales. Just two years later new Caetano-bodied Volvos VC8-12 displaced PD36-40 and 60 from these duties. *Jonathan McDonnell*

Bus Éireann Eurolines-liveried VC33 traverses Birmingham city centre dressed for service 894 in August 1996. *Jonathan McDonnell*

Without question, this coach operated the longest ever Bus Éireann/CIE route. Participating in the Eurolines system, for three summer seasons (June to August during 1997-9), VC79 covered a weekly return trip to and from Stuttgart on service 876. It worked opposite a German coach travelling in the opposite direction. For the first year when new, Bus Éireann drivers placed it 'shipside' onto a ferry at Dublin and contractor KMP of North Wales provided two drivers to bring it 'double-headed' from Holyhead docks via Birmingham, then by-passing London by use of the M25 motorway and then onwards to Frankfurt via Dover, Calais, Brussels and Cologne. Because of tachograph limitations, the portion from Frankfurt to Stuttgart via Mannheim was covered by a German driver from the Touring company in Frankfurt. The German-based coach was also Touring-operated. During the first year, 1997, VC79 started and finished in Galway. For necessary practical reasons, it was fitted with both a toilet and special air-conditioning facilities which could be serviced at the Thermo King production plant in Ballybrit, Galway. For 1998 and 1999, two Broadstone-based Bus Éireann drivers took the coach to and from Frankfurt with the German driver continuing onwards from there. In 2000, VP80 displaced VC79 from the role.

The picture, taken on 1 August 1998, when two of this book's authors travelled the complete return trip, shows VC79, framed by the Calais 7 docking gantry, about to arrive on French soil. Inset shows a detailed view of the windscreen running board.

Since autumn 1999, VC79 has served as a spare Express coach and worked a cross-section of local services from Broadstone and Waterford. Its on-board toilet has been removed, so it now has seating for 53 passengers. *Both Ian Molloy*

Left: In August 1998, VC79 poses beside a tram in Frankfurt whilst *en route* from Stuttgart to Dublin. It was a quiet Sunday morning and the tram driver was happy to pause for this unusual photo. *Jonathan McDonnell*

Above: SP89 is one of a pair, SP90 being the other, of tri-axle coaches for *Eurolines* services. They are being used on southern cross-channel services linking Cork, Limerick and Waterford with London. SP89 is seen here in the newly refurbished bus station in Cork on route 890. These tri-axle coaches give enhanced stability when negotiating tight corners, especially on the roads in Pembrokeshire in Wales. *Darren Hall*

Appendix: Bus Eireann Fleet Lists

Schools 1 February 1987

Type	SF	SS	CS	Total
	43	740	71	854
%	5.0	86.7	8.3	100
Year	1983	1967-73	1965/6	
Age*	4	14-20	21-2	

*at Feb 1987 (years)

Schools 5 September 2006

Type	AD	AS	BS	DA	DVH	ES	KS	LS	MH	ML	OP	P	PD	PL	SI	TE	VC	VP	Total
	43	5	5	9	17	5	78	179	27	8	25	39	57	59	22	33	50	23	**684**
%	6.3	0.7	0.7	1.3	2.5	0.7	11.4	26.2	3.9	1.2	3.7	5.7	8.3	8.6	3.2	4.8	7.3	3.4	100
Year	1994	2006	2006	1993	1993	2006	1985-7	1988-92	1999	1997	1997-9	1993	1990-2	1990/1	2000-2	1988/9	1994-2000	2000/1/2	
Age*	12	0	0	13	13	0	19-21	14-8	7	9	7-9	13	14-6	15-6	4-6	17-8	6-12	4-6	

*at Sep 2006 (years)

Service 1 February 1987

Type	M	MD	MG	D	DF	KC	KD	KE	KR	KS	CVH	EVH	LVH	WVH	HB	Total
	30	60	70	26	1	82	26	51	221	1	19	28	5	3	1	624
%	4.8	9.6	11.2	4.2	0.2	13.1	4.2	8.2	35.4	0.2	3.0	4.5	0.8	0.5	0.2	100
Year	1971-2	1971-2	1971-2	1973-5	1975	1983-5	1981-3	1981	1985-7	1983	1986	1986	1963	1963	1966	
Age*	15-16	15-16	15-16	12-14	12	2-4	4-6	6	0-2	4	1	1	24	24	21	

*at Feb 1987 (years)

Service 5 September 2006

Type	DD	DPC	DWM	DWR	MC	ME	MH	ML	OT	SC	SP	SR	SW	VC	VG	VNC	VP	VR	VW	VWL	VWM	To
	23	42	15	20	20	10	4	2	1	71	90	52	2	131	20	1	47	54	9	43	8	66
%	3.5	6.3	2.3	3.0	3.0	1.5	0.6	0.3	0.2	10.7	13.5	7.8	0.3	19.7	3.0	0.2	7.1	8.1	1.4	6.5	1.2	
Year	2002/4	2000/2	2000	2001	2000	1997	1999	1997	1998	2001/4	2005/6	2001/2/4	1998, 2002	1994-2003	2004	1993	2000	2000	1997	1997-2004	2000	
Age*	2-4	4-6	6	5	6	9	7	9	8	2-5	0-1	2-5	4-8	3-12	2	13	6	6	9	2-9	6	

*at Sep 2006 (years)